Journeying with Hope into a New Year

Journeying with Hope into a New Year

Reflections for Advent and Christmas

PAUL R. DEKAR

RESOURCE *Publications* · Eugene, Oregon

JOURNEYING WITH HOPE INTO A NEW YEAR
Reflections for Advent and Christmas

Resource Publications
An Imprint of Wipf and Stock Publishers
199 W. 8th Ave., Suite 3
Eugene, OR 97401

www.wipfandstock.com

PAPERBACK ISBN: 978-1-5326-5904-1
HARDCOVER ISBN: 978-1-5326-5905-8
EBOOK ISBN: 978-1-5326-5906-5

07/26/22

And now here is my secret, a very simple secret: It is only with the heart that one can see rightly; what is essential is invisible to the eye.

Voici mon secret. Il est très simple: on ne voit bien qu'avec le cœur. L'essentiel est invisible pour les yeux.

No se ve bien sino con el corazón. Lo esencial es invisible a los ojos.

ANTOINE DE SAINT-EXUPÉRY, *THE LITTLE PRINCE*

Contents

Contents

Introduction

JOURNEYING WITH HOPE INTO a New Year: Reflections for Advent and Christmas has its origins in 1982, when our family lived at an ecumenical institute between Jerusalem and Bethlehem. My wife Nancy and I wrote a letter highlighting our experience of Christmastide in the Holy Land. Inspired by writing this message from afar, we have continued annually to share family news, a moving quote from a hymn or literary work and spiritual reflections.

In writing this book, I seek to reach a wider audience and to build on a practice of many Christians, individually or with others, to observe the period beginning four Sundays before Christmas as Advent. I hope readers will use these meditations daily through December. Each one includes a biblical text, a brief reflection and a prayer. For example, in the fourth entry I quote Isaiah 9: 6 in which the Hebrew prophet writes of a savior to be called Wonderful Counselor, Mighty God, Everlasting Father and Prince of Peace. Centuries later, a time similarly marked by conflict and need for respite, readers may resonate with Isaiah and pray for peace.

As we begin our journey, I open with an epigraph citing *The Little Prince* by Antoine de Saint-Exupéry: "And now here is my secret, a very simple secret: It is only with the heart that one can see rightly; what is essential is invisible to the eye." Though no single line from non-biblical literature can adequately summarize the meditations that follow, Saint-Exupéry gets to the heart of why we celebrate Christmas, to magnify the One who came that we might have life, and have it abundantly." (John 10:10)

Writing in early 2022, I am aware that people around the world are living through a time of many challenges including worsening climate change, growing economic uncertainties and systemic racism. Wars have led to unprecedented numbers of displaced persons and refugees. Many readers will have lost loved ones and friends to Covid-19.

One can identify with those who want to hunker down, leaving it to politicians, business leaders or charitable agencies to tackle such problems. Alternatively, one can recognize that, as individuals, along with our communities, nations and global organizations, we have power to influence the course of events in positive ways.

In the *Bible*, Matthew provides an example in the story of the flight of Jesus with his parents to Egypt to avoid the massacre of innocents ordered by Herod. At the time when Jesus was born, over a million Jews lived in Egypt. Many like Jesus and His family were refugees. Two thousand years later, millions recount the story of Jesus the refugee and seek to follow Him.

During the first week, meditations 1–7 explore the promise of a Messiah in Hebrew Scripture. Some New Testament writers cite these ancient texts. During the second week, meditations 8–16 highlight passages about Jesus' birth. The remaining meditations focus on key teachings of Jesus. We conclude on New Years' Eve with personal wishes and intentions.

By mentioning practices that Nancy and I have observed such as cutting a Christmas tree at a local farm, lighting candles on an Advent wreath or undertaking a retreat, I have offered illustrative ideas from personal experience. Unless otherwise noted, I draw on the New Revised Standard version of the *Bible* and *The Presbyterian Hymnal: Hymns, Psalms, and Spiritual Songs*. A list of suggestions for further reading includes sources consulted, Christmas stories for children and contact information for monasteries and retreat centers mentioned in the text.

"Blessed are Those Who Mourn" draws on a December 19, 2021 "Blue Holiday" service at McNeill Baptist Church in Hamilton, Ontario. Jenn Nettleton wrote the litany. The original author of the prayer is unknown. "Love One Another" first appeared in a

Baptist Peace Fellowship of North America booklet, *Think on These Things. Meditations for December.*

In the final reflection, I recall a simple practice His Holiness Tenzen Gyatzo, the fourteenth Dalai Lama and exiled leader of Tibetan Buddhism, the Dalai Lama, shared on the eve of a new millennium. He hoped the exercise would increase love and compassion in the world. Re-read on the eve of a new year, the questions are simple, inspiring and helpful. The practice of cherishing the earth and all its beings can be transformative.

I am grateful for ideas shared by Nancy Dekar, Eyleen Farmer, Ross Lawford and Ron Morissey. They are not responsible for errors in the text. Writing with attention to gender, I do not change biblical texts or quotes even when not inclusive. I trust the original author would use non-gender specific prose were she or he writing in our times. Photographs are my own.

I close this opening reflection with a prayer by the Cistercian monk Thomas Merton. You may listen to this prayer as sung by Kate Campbell during the 2007 meeting in Memphis of the International Thomas Merton Society. The prayer originally appeared in *Thoughts in Solitude*, as follows:

> My Lord God, I have no idea where I am going. I do not see the road ahead of me. I cannot know for certain where it will end. Nor do I really know myself, and the fact that I think that I am following your will does not mean that I am actually doing so. But I believe that the desire to please you does in fact please you. And I hope I have that desire in all that I am doing. I hope that I will never do anything apart from that desire. And I know that if I do this you will lead me by the right road though I may know nothing about it. Therefore will I trust you always though I may seem to be lost and in the shadow of death. I will not fear, for you are ever with me, and you will never leave me to face my perils alone.

1

Prepare the Way of the Lord

A voice cries out: "In the wilderness prepare the way of the
Lord, make straight in the desert a highway for our God.
Every valley shall be lifted up, and every mountain and hill
be made low; the uneven ground shall become level, and
the rough places a plain. Then the glory of the Lord shall be
revealed, and all people shall see it together, for the mouth of
the Lord has spoken." Isaiah 40:3–5

The beginning of the good news of Jesus Christ, the Son of
God. As it is written in the prophet Isaiah, "See, I am sending
my messenger ahead of you, who will prepare your way; the
voice of one crying out in the wilderness: 'Prepare the way of
the Lord, make his paths straight.'" Mark 1:1–3

TODAY'S TEXTS FROM THE Old Testament book of Isaiah and the
New Testament book of Mark included a call to prepare the way of
the Lord with an exhortation to righteous living. Written some six
centuries before Jesus' birth, the Isaiah passage originated immedi-
ately before the conquest of Jerusalem. Isaiah anticipated a joyous
restoration of the Jewish people to their homes and the mission of
a "suffering servant" who will record God's teaching and restore
justice and peace to the world.

The gospel, or message according to Mark, generally regarded as the earliest of the four biblical accounts of Jesus' life and teachings, opened with the activity of John the Baptist. The prophet appeared in the wilderness proclaiming a baptism of repentance for the forgiveness of sins. At the time, John's preaching was considered radical and dangerous and would eventually lead to imprisonment and death. However, this did not end his influence but rather heightened expectancy of our Lord's birth. Many of those who heard John proclaim "one is more powerful than I is coming after me" saw Jesus as the one who would establish God's realm on earth.

How might we prepare the way of the Lord? This Advent, we can shift gears, draw into ourselves and our circle of family and friends, rekindle our spirits and take an inventory of our lives. Reading and meditating on today's texts can stimulate our imagination about that time when the glory of God is revealed and renew our expectation of the earthquake-like spiritual stirring resulting from the birth of Jesus.

Prayer: God, just as You withdraw sleep from our eyes each morning, grant us wakefulness that we may see Your glory, praise You and live in the manner John the baptizer called for, and Jesus lived and died. Amen.

2

Emmanuel, God with Us

Therefore the Lord himself will give you a sign. Look, the young woman is with child and shall bear a son, and shall name him Immanuel. Isaiah 7:14

"Look, the virgin shall conceive and bear a son, and they shall name him Emmanuel," which means, "God is with us." Matthew 1:23

EMMANUEL IS THE NAME the prophet Isaiah gave the child foretold as a sign to the king of ancient Israel and his court that God would save them from their enemies. In the first of the four biblical accounts of Jesus' life and teachings, Matthew adopts the name. It means that God is with us.

In good times, or naught, God is with us. Could there be any greater words of comfort? A popular story entitled "Footprints in the Sand" expresses this idea. In a dream, one is walking along a beach and notices footprints in the sand. Sometimes there are two sets of footprints; other times there is only one. On this occasion, a time of personal crisis, the beachcomber prays to Jesus complaining that He had promised always to walk alongside. Why when needed most, was Jesus not present?

Jesus responded that He would never, ever leave anyone alone. When there is only one set of footprints, He has carried the one in need.

This story encapsulates the idea that God knows what we require, hears our prayers and is always with us. Though we might not be able to experience, confirm or accept God's ways, God is always with us. A common phrase, "I've got your back" applies in the sense that God watches out for us in ways we might otherwise miss.

Prayer: "Holy One, hear our prayer and grant us Your peace. Amen." Psalm 143:1

3

Darkness and Light

The people who walked in darkness have seen a great light;
those who lived in a land of deep darkness, on them light has
shined. Isaiah 9: 2

Again Jesus spoke to them, saying, "I am the light of the world.
Whoever follows me will never walk in darkness but will have
the light of life." John 8:12

IN MANY SERVICES OF worship, lighting a candle on an Advent wreath or Christmas tree is a sign of expectation and hope. For many years, Nancy and I were members of MacNeill Baptist Church in Hamilton, Ontario, Canada. On each of the four Sundays before Christmas, someone–generally a young person–lit a candle and read a text highlighting one of four themes: hope, faith, joy and peace. On Christmas Eve or Christmas Day, a young person lit a fifth candle. This was the Christ candle that highlighted Jesus as the light of the world.

During the service of worship, participants shared joys and concerns. The liturgist incorporated these into the congregational prayers. The full blaze of all five candles symbolized the fulfillment of the promise of Isaiah that a great light would shine on those living in dark times and of John, that with Jesus, we never walk in darkness but in the light of life.

As I write in early 2022, I am aware some readers, due to personal losses or needs, may be experiencing great darkness and little light. What challenges are you facing on your journey? How might a tradition like lighting candles on an Advent wreath speak to you? Can the words of Isaiah and John or the illumination of five candles speak to your condition and need?

Prayer: God, may we find hope in the biblical witness that people who walked in darkness have seen a great light; and have the light of life. As we prepare to join in celebrating the birth of Jesus, Light of the world, may we find hope in the rhythm of darkness and light. Amen.

4

Prince of Peace

For a child has been born for us, a son given to us; authority rests upon his shoulders; and he is named Wonderful
Counselor, Mighty God, Everlasting Father, Prince of Peace.

Isaiah 9:6

IN HEBREW SCRIPTURE, THE word prince identifies royalty, a son
who will become king. A daughter or princess is equally worthy of
recognition. In today's reading from the prophet Isaiah, the Messiah is to be the prince of princes, the ruler who inaugurates God's
reign.

Nearly three thousand years ago, Isaiah envisioned a future
without war, a time when God's people live righteously in accord
with God's promises. Likewise in Judges 6: 24, God was named
Peace.

Many readers of this meditation may recognize Isaiah 9:6 as
sung in the choral work *Messiah* by George Frederic Handel. Originally performed in Dublin, Ireland around Easter on April 13, 1742,
readers may enjoy listening to a recording of this magnificent and
uplifting work. How does this music, written in much earlier times,
or the birth of a child two thousand years ago have significance in
the twenty-first century? In what way might a child born so long
ago be celebrated as the one to be called Wonderful Counselor,
Mighty God, Everlasting Father, and Prince of Peace? What might

we do to realize a society that more closely resembles this biblical vision of peace than is currently the case? What is needed to realize the coming reign of God?

In words of a popular choral work, *Dona Nobis Pacem*, let us pray that Jesus, Prince of Peace, might come and fill our hearts with peace. Amen.

5

Glory of God

Arise, shine; for your light has come, and the glory of the Lord has risen upon you. For darkness shall cover the earth, and thick darkness the peoples; but the Lord will arise upon you, and his glory will appear over you. Nations shall come to your light and kings to the brightness of your dawn. Isaiah 60:1–3

God chose to make known how great among the Gentiles are the riches of the glory of this mystery, which is Christ in you, the hope of glory. Colossians 1:27

IN THE *BIBLE*, THE glory of God is associated with brightness and light that is a result of the presence of God. As early as the book of Genesis, the glory of God is revealed in the act of creation. In Exodus, God speaks to Moses through a burning bush. Yes, God can be manifest through a burning bush because nothing, not even a plant, is devoid of God.

Isaiah and other Jewish prophets anticipated that the glory of God would be revealed through a Savior. For Paul writing to the early Christian community in Colossae, a town in what is now Turkey, Jesus was the Savior who manifested the glory of God to all humanity.

How is God present in your life? How does Jesus brighten your life? Can you recall a specific person or event through which you have experienced the glory of God? How might you thank God afresh today?

As we close today's time of meditation, let us recall words of Meister Eckhart, a Medieval Christian mystic, who wrote that it is sufficient if the only prayer one ever says throughout life is thank you.

Prayer: Creator God, thank you for Your glory. Thank you for Jesus, Creator, Redeemer and Sustaining presence. Amen.

6

Dream of God

The Lord spoke to Moses on Mount Sinai, saying.. . . When
you enter the land that I am giving you, the land shall observe
a Sabbath for the Lord. Six years you shall sow your field,
and six years you shall prune your vineyard, and gather in
their yield; but in the seventh year there shall be a Sabbath
of complete rest for the land, a Sabbath for the Lord: you
shall not sow your field or prune your vineyard. You shall not
reap the aftergrowth of your harvest or gather the grapes of
your unpruned vine: it shall be a year of complete rest for the
land. You may eat what the land yields during its Sabbath . . .
[and] on the Day of Atonement—you shall have the trumpet
sounded throughout all your land. And you shall hallow the
fiftieth year and you shall proclaim liberty throughout the
land to all its inhabitants. It shall be a Jubilee for you . . . it
shall be holy to you. . . Leviticus 25:1–12

ACCORDING TO GENESIS 2:15, God placed Adam and Eve in Eden,
a garden that individuals could tend and where they could enjoy
the fruits of their labor. However, because of the disobedience of
these first humans, God drove them from Eden. This symbolized
the broken relationship between God and humans. Subsequently,

much of the *Bible* described God's efforts to restore humans to life in harmony with God and the created order.

Writers of the *Bible* used diverse representations of Eden restored. Images such as peaceable kingdom (Isaiah 11:1–9); new creation (2 Corinthians 5:17), new heaven and earth (Isaiah 65:17–19) and Jubilee (Leviticus 25:1–12) have inspired individuals and movements. For example, in the early 1980s, a British "Do They Know It's Christmas?" project inspired entertainer and social activist Harry Belafonte to organize recording of a song, "We Are the World." All the best-known music artists of the day participated, raising relief aid for starving people in Africa.

Similarly, in 2000, organizers of the Jubilee Movement cited the Leviticus text as a theological basis for an international campaign to relieve the debts of poor nations. In 2005, organizers of the "Make Poverty History" campaign sought to increase awareness and pressure governments into taking actions towards relieving absolute poverty.

Today, we highlight a similar effort. "Dream of God" is the title of a book by Verna J. Dozier. A secondary school teacher and Episcopal religious educator, Dozier characterized the dream of God as reconciling rebellious humans to the Creator and creation. Nancy and I first read her book as part of a servant leadership group in Memphis, Tennessee inspired by The Church of the Saviour in Washington, D. C. As we reflected on Dozier's book, we sought to incorporate her ideas in our journeys inward (prayer and meditation) and outward (worship and using our gifts in community service).

Such campaigns and prophets like Isaiah, Micah or Verna Dozier challenge humans to be midwives of the dream of God. Indeed, this is how I see my role in writing this book. Not experienced as a medical midwife, I sincerely pray that these meditations encourage readers to share in birthing the dream of God.

Adapting words of the Leviticus text, the contemporary songwriter Mary Chapin Carpenter sings of Jubilee on her album *Stones on the Rock*. Can you imagine you are like a frail boat on a vast sea scanning the night for a great guiding light that announces the day of Jubilee? How might you midwife birthing God's dream?

Prayer: Loving God, I acknowledge that I am frail. Thank You for forgiving me. By Your Spirit, enable me to live in accord with Your dream that all people live in right relationship with You, one another and all creation. May I contribute to realizing Your day of Jubilee. Amen.

7

He Shall Purify

See, I am sending my messenger to prepare the way before
me, and the Lord whom you seek will suddenly come to
his temple. The messenger of the covenant in whom you
delight—indeed, he is coming, says the Lord of hosts. But who
can endure the day of his coming, and who can stand when
he appears? For he is like a refiner's fire and like fullers' soap;
he will sit as a refiner and purifier of silver, and he will purify
the descendants of Levi and refine them like gold and silver,
until they present offerings to the Lord in righteousness.
Malachi 3:1–3

ALL SOCIETIES HAVE LAWS that regulate the way people live. Such
codes for organizing life are in part utilitarian, to keep away de-
mons, germs or malfeasants. They also contribute to the right or-
dering of the community.

Many societies have purity laws as part of their sacred texts.
The holiness codes and dietary restrictions of Hebrew scripture are
examples. Similarly, between 1921 and 1933, Amendment Eighteen
to the United States Constitution prohibited the manufacture, sale
or transportation of intoxicating beverages within, importing such
into, or exporting alcohol from the United States and all territory
subject to its jurisdiction.

In a book entitled *Purity and Danger*, anthropologist Mary Douglas showed how purity laws can serve a positive role by ensuring the cohesion of a society. Purity laws can also function in more negative ways for some members. For example, traditional India organizes society by a system according to which those who deal with substances regarded by upper castes as impure—manure, meat, leather, bodily waste—are ranked more lowly in the social hierarchy.

Writing several centuries before the birth of Jesus, the prophet known as Malachi envisioned a forerunner who would challenge the people of Israel to remain faithful to their covenant with God, and a Savior who would purify them. George Frederic Handel's English-language *The Messiah* included today's text. Performance of this choral work has become a beloved Advent custom celebrating Jesus the Messiah who shattered all barriers that divide people and who continues to inspire believers to follow His way.

I invite you to close with a prayer from *The Oxford Book of Prayer* by George Appleton, former Anglican Bishop of Jerusalem. "O God of many names, lover of all nations, we pray for peace in our hearts, in our homes, in our nations, in our world, the peace of Your will, the peace of our need. Amen."

8

The Birth of Jesus Foretold

In the sixth month the angel Gabriel was sent by God to a
town in Galilee called Nazareth, to a virgin engaged to a man
whose name was Joseph, of the house of David. The virgin's
name was Mary. And he came to her and said, "Greetings,
favored one! The Lord is with you." But she was much per-
plexed by his words and pondered what sort of greeting this
might be. The angel said to her, "Do not be afraid, Mary, for
you have found favor with God. And now, you will conceive
in your womb and bear a son, and you will name him Jesus.
He will be great, and will be called the Son of the Most High,
and the Lord God will give to him the throne of his ancestor
David. He will reign over the house of Jacob forever, and of
his kingdom there will be no end." Mary said to the angel,
"How can this be, since I am a virgin?" The angel said to her,
"The Holy Spirit will come upon you, and the power of the
Most High will overshadow you; therefore the child to be
born will be holy; he will be called Son of God. And now,
your relative Elizabeth in her old age has also conceived a
son; and this is the sixth month for her who was said to be
barren. For nothing will be impossible with God." Then Mary

said, "Here am I, the servant of the Lord; let it be with me according to your word." Then the angel departed from her.

Luke 1:26–38

AMONG NEW TESTAMENT AUTHORS, only Matthew and Luke write of Jesus' conception by the Holy Spirit. In today's text, Mary asks "How can this be, since I am a virgin?" Over the centuries, much ink has been written about the virgin birth of Jesus. Is Mary's virginity the most crucial point for Luke? Or that Mary had found favor with God and would bear the Son of God?

Paul, an early convert, sought to assure early Christian communities to which he wrote that God was with them. In Colossians 1:17, Paul affirmed that in Jesus Christ is before all things, and in Him all things hold together. In Romans 8:38–39, Paul wrote that nothing, neither death, nor life, nor angels, nor rulers, nor things present, nor things to come, nor powers, nor height, nor depth, nor anything else in all creation, can separate us from the love of God in Christ Jesus our Lord.

Similarly in history, extraordinary Christians—some of whom we call saints—have shared their faith in times of distress or uncertainty. As an example, in her "Showings," Julian of Norwich, a fourteenth-century nun, related that she had suffered a serious illness. In the span of a few hours God assured her that all would be well, and that all manner of things would be well.

How might the angel's words to a peasant, "Do not be afraid," Paul's letters to early Christian communities or words of a fourteenth-century recluse be helpful to you? Does Luke's story reassure you at a time when there are many reasons to fear? How do you face challenges?

Prayer: Jesus, You came among us, journeyed with fellow humans through Your brief life and abide with us beyond the grave through eternity. We thank You that all shall be well, and all manner of things shall be well. Amen.

9

The Genealogy of Jesus

Jesus was about thirty years old when he began his work.
He was the son (as was thought) of Joseph son of Heli, son
of Matthat, son of Levi, son of Melchi, son of Jannai, son of
Joseph, son of Mattathias, son of Amos, son of Nahum, son
of Esli, son of Naggai, son of Maath, son of Mattathias, son of
Semein, son of Josech, son of Joda, son of Joanan, son of Rhesa,
son of Zerubbabel, son of Shealtiel, son of Neri, son of Melchi,
son of Addi, son of Cosam, son of Elmadam, son of Er, son
of Joshua, son of Eliezer, son of Jorim, son of Matthat, son of
Levi, son of Simeon, son of Judah, son of Joseph, son of Jonam,
son of Eliakim, son of Melea, son of Menna, son of Mattatha,
son of Nathan, son of David, son of Jesse, son of Obed, son of
Boaz, son of Sala, son of Nahshon, son of Amminadab, son of
Admin, son of Arni, son of Hezron, son of Perez, son of Judah,
son of Jacob, son of Isaac, son of Abraham, son of Terah, son of
Nahor, son of Serug, son of Reu, son of Peleg, son of Eber, son
of Shelah, son of Cainan, son of Arphaxad, son of Shem, son
of Noah, son of Lamech, son of Methuselah, son of Enoch, son
of Jared, son of Mahalaleel, son of Cainan, son of Enos, son of
Seth, son of Adam, son of God. Luke 3:23–38

The Genealogy of Jesus

Today, we reflect on the family lineage of Jesus. There are differences in the accounts of Jesus' background by Matthew, Mark, Luke and John. Matthew lists Jesus' ancestors chronologically forward from Abraham to the nativity. Mark begins the good news of Jesus Christ by naming him as the Son of God. Luke traces Jesus' family linage retrospectively from Joseph to the creation of humankind in the image of God. John opens more theologically.

The genealogy of Jesus as recorded in Matthew 1: 1–17 is notable for including four women—Tamar, Rahab, Ruth and Mary—in the genealogy of Jesus. Women are absent in Luke's account. We may account for such differences by noting that Matthew and Luke had varied backgrounds, points of view and readership in mind. Matthew, a Jew, may have wanted to emphasize Jesus' birth as the fulfillment of ancient promises. Luke, a non-Jew, may have wanted to emphasize the significance of Jesus's birth for everyone, not simply the people Israel.

Despite such discrepancies, we may consider that it is more noteworthy to recognize that Luke traces Jesus' family back to the first human, Adam, son of God. For Luke, Jesus was a man, fully human with every person. This was consistent with God's original plan for creation.

Against all odds, and perhaps even in the face of modern scientific skepticism, can you journey through this Advent grateful to God for the mystery of Jesus' conception and birth? Can you join in another prayer adapted from Bishop Appleton's *Jerusalem Prayers*?

Glory be to You, O Lord our God, in the mystery of Your being, in the creation of the universe, in Your incarnation in Jesus Christ, in the availability of Your Spirit for everyone, in all the truth, love and goodness that we find about us, in Your touch upon our souls and in Your will for all humanity. Glory be to You, O Lord our God. Amen.

10

Everyone a You

> And Mary said, "My soul magnifies the Lord, and my spirit
> rejoices in God my Savior. For he has looked with favor on
> the lowliness of his servant . . .. He has brought down the
> powerful from their thrones, and lifted up the lowly; he has
> filled the hungry with good things, and sent the rich away
> empty." Luke 1:46, 53

MARY'S POEM, OFTEN CALLED "The Magnificat," followed a meeting
of Mary with her relative Elizabeth. At that time, Mary was preg-
nant with Jesus, Elizabeth with John the Baptist. Mary expressed
her joy. Elizabeth acknowledged the news saying, "Blessed are you
among women, and blessed be the fruit of your womb." (Luke 1:41).

Mary dared to believe that God, her Savior, had favored her.
She bore, and gave birth to Jesus, who brings salvation to the world.
Her "Magnificat" expresses a key idea that for God, we all matter. God loves the poor, sends away the rich and calls workers for
peace daughters and sons. Despite the crass commercialism that at
times threatens to overwhelm us this season, the truth of Mary's
song shines through: in God's eyes, everyone is a you and not an
impersonal it.

Monastic communities of all denominations and many congregations repeat Mary's words, often at the end of the day. Recordings

abound. Around the world, the poor especially identify with Mary, a lowly peasant woman whom God chose to be the mother of Jesus, and sing or chant her song.

You may be reading this on December 10. On this day in 1948, the member states of the United Nations declared that every human being has inalienable rights. Many governments have not lived up to this resolve. There are many ways to respond to this tragedy. We can pray. We can inform ourselves. We can support organizations like Amnesty International and write letters on behalf of victims of human rights violations. We can join in sponsoring a refugee. By working to protect the life, liberty and security of every person, we follow in the footsteps of Jesus, Prince of Peace.

Prayer: God, thank You for the humble origins of Jesus. As we prepare to celebrate the birth of our Savior, grant that we may recognize that in Your eyes, everyone is a you and not an it. No one is excluded from Your love. Amen.

11

The Birth of Jesus

In those days a decree went out from Emperor Augustus that
all the world should be registered. This was the first registration and was taken while Quirinius was governor of Syria.
All went to their own towns to be registered. Joseph also
went from the town of Nazareth in Galilee to Judea, to the
city of David called Bethlehem, because he was descended
from the house and family of David. He went to be registered
with Mary, to whom he was engaged and who was expecting a child. While they were there, the time came for her to
deliver her child. And she gave birth to her firstborn son and
wrapped him in bands of cloth, and laid him in a manger,
because there was no place for them in the inn. Luke 2:1–7

IN JEWISH SCRIPTURE, BETHLEHEM was home to several historical
figures, notably Ruth and David. At the time of Jesus' birth, Bethlehem was on a major trade route between Hebron to the north and
the Negev desert to the south.

The evangelists Luke, Matthew and John located the birth of
Jesus in a Bethlehem stable. In the year 325 of the Common Era,
the Roman emperor Constantine erected a church at the purported
site of Jesus' birth. After its destruction, a sixth-century emperor

named Justinian built a new and larger church that is the foundation for the present structure.

Today, were a reader literally to journey from Jerusalem to Bethlehem, one would pass flocks of sheep, olive groves and Israeli settlements. One would need to navigate Israeli security checks before reaching what remains a small town populated primarily by Palestinians.

Bethlehem has an abundance of shops. Merchants sell various items carved from olive wood, including a manger scene called a crèche. Every year, on the first Sunday in Advent, Nancy and I reassemble the crèche we purchased during our year in the Holy Land. We wonder how its Palestinian carver has fared since our visit to the city.

In a pamphlet entitled *Bethlehem Revisited*, Quaker Douglas Steere writes that the Advent season is a time when Christians are invited to Bethlehem and to reconsider its "cosmic significance." He reflects as follows,

> I cannot see the life of Jesus as other than God trying to disclose his love for us and his attempt, at any price, to show us that the cosmos is grounded in love. All hate, all sin, all discord, all clefts, all ignorance, all confusion will finally give way to love. But this love, like a strip of wood, has its grain which must be followed. If we follow this grain we will find that we must change the patterns in which we have previously cast our lives. And I do not see how God could have made this disclosure more effectively than by placing his love in the body of a child.

Does the lowly birth of Jesus have "cosmic significance" for you? How do the life and teachings of Jesus offer hope to a friend or community at a time of personal need?

Prayer: God, we give thanks for the love shown in Jesus. We commit ourselves to love through Jesus Christ, our Lord. Amen.

12

No Room in the Inn

In those days a decree went out from Emperor Augustus that all the world should be registered. This was the first registration and was taken while Quirinius was governor of Syria. All went to their own towns to be registered. Joseph also went from the town of Nazareth in Galilee to Judea, to the city of David called Bethlehem, because he was descended from the house and family of David. He went to be registered with Mary, to whom he was engaged and who was expecting a child. While they were there, the time came for her to deliver her child. And she gave birth to her firstborn son and wrapped him in bands of cloth, and laid him in a manger, because there was no place for them in the inn. Luke 2:1–7

YESTERDAY, WE CONSIDERED THE cosmic significance of the birth of Jesus. Today, re-reading Luke's account, we highlight that there was no vacancy for the family in the local inn.

Mary and Joseph were forced to journey to Bethlehem due to a census or tax mandated by the oppressive Roman rulers of Palestine. Thus in the later days of Mary's pregnancy, the couple had to travel some ninety miles (hundred and fifty kilometers) from Nazareth in northern Palestine to Bethlehem near Jerusalem. In biblical times, such a trip likely would have required several days. By contrast in modern Israel, one can drive that distance on a modern highway in about ninety minutes not counting stops at security check points.

Had Joseph chosen not to register or pay the tax, the Romans could have forced the couple off their land since at this time concepts like human rights or progressive taxation simply did not exist. Administrators of Roman rule prospered. The poor masses suffered. Is it any wonder that, a few years after Jesus' birth, the territory convulsed in a Jewish revolt against Roman rule?

Arriving in Bethlehem, Joseph and Mary numbered among a throng of weary travelers looking for lodging. Finding no room in the local inn, they made do. Mary gave birth to Jesus in a barn surrounded by animals.

Have you experienced any circumstance that allows you to identify with the young couple? For example, have you ever driven on an interstate or interprovincial highway and, after a long day on the road, exited to seek a motel only to find no vacancy signs? Or, stranded by a storm or natural disaster, had to stay in a community shelter among strangers? What did you do?

Prayer: May Jesus, first born in a stable, be born in me afresh today. Amen.

13

Peace on Earth, Good Will toward Humanity

> An Angel of the Lord . . . said to them, "Do not be afraid, for
> see—I am bringing you good news of great joy for all the
> people: to you this day in the city of David a Savior, who is the
> Messiah, the Lord. This will be a sign for you: you will find a
> child wrapped in bands of cloth and lying in a manger." And
> suddenly there was with the angel a multitude of the heavenly
> host, praising God and saying, "Glory to God in the highest
> heaven, and on earth peace among those whom he favors."
> Luke 2:9–15

CHRISTMAS CARDS AND CAROLS frequently include this pronounce-
ment to shepherds tending their flocks on the first Christmas Eve
that Jesus' birth will initiate a time of peace and good will on earth
for all humanity. With this announcement, a multitude of angels
appeared, praising God and saying, "Glory to God in the highest
heaven, and on earth peace to those on whom he favors." Readers
may be familiar with the well-known Christmas carol, "It Came
Upon the Midnight Clear," whose words, "Peace on the earth, good
will to all from heaven's all gracious King" derive from today's text.

At this time, however, readers may well feel quite overwhelmed by the current state of the world, which seems not only far from peaceful but rife with dangers and uncertainties. Readers can identify with those who hunker down, leaving it to politicians, business leaders or non-government leaders to tackle pressing social concerns.

In 1965, similarly overwhelmed by the peacemaking work to which he had been called, a young American activist Jim Forest wrote a letter to the widely published and socially conscious monk Thomas Merton. Replying, Merton encouraged Forest to trust God and to do God's will.

In these equally troubling times, I pray that readers can trust that God is making peace out of all that is happening, and that you can make a difference. In Jesus' name. Amen.

14

What Gift Can We Give?

When they had heard the king, they set out; and there, ahead
of them, went the star that they had seen at its rising, until
it stopped over the place where the child was. When they
saw that the star had stopped, they were overwhelmed with
joy. On entering the house, they saw the child with Mary his
mother, and they knelt down and paid him homage. Then,
opening their treasure chests, they offered him gifts of gold,
frankincense and myrrh. Matthew 2:9–12

IN A CHRISTMAS MEDITATION, the sixteenth-century Protestant
Reformer Martin Luther recalled the story of the three wise men.
Drawn by a brilliant star to seek a great king, they found Jesus with
his parents in a stable where the Church of the Nativity now stands.
However, disappointed by what they found, the three travelers left
for home. Shortly afterwards, they were overwhelmed with a sense
of guilt, for they had judged God by human standards.

Thus the three wise men turned back toward Bethlehem, but
they soon despaired all the more, for their guiding star had faded,
causing them to lose their way. Miraculously, when they stopped
at a well to quench their thirst, the image of the lost star still shone
and guided them back to the tumbled down shack where, in Luther's words, they found a poor young mother with a little babe,

most unlike a mighty king. Nevertheless, the wise men did not turn back, but in great, strong faith, fell on their knees, worshipped Jesus and presented their treasures.

A favorite carol, "All poor ones and humble," celebrates the rich gifts the three wise men gave the newborn child. Even the oxen in the stable shared their hay with baby Jesus. Our gifts, though, do not have to be as regal. However modest, we fill our days during Advent with many joy-filled activities. Personal examples abound such as erecting a crèche, decorating a tree, sending a card, writing a seasonal letter, or caroling. Acknowledging that, for some, the season is challenging, we may participate in a Blue Holiday Service.

How do we replicate the journey of the three sojourners from the East to the site of Jesus' birth? What gift might we give to the one who has come to set us free?

Prayer: Jesus, your nativity has revealed the Light of wisdom, for in it those who looked to the stars were drawn to your birthplace, where they worshiped You. All praise to You, O Lord. Amen.

15

Flight to Egypt

Now after they had left, an angel of the Lord appeared to
Joseph in a dream and said, "Get up, take the child and his
mother, and flee to Egypt, and remain there until I tell you; for
Herod is about to search for the child, to destroy him." Then
Joseph got up, took the child and his mother by night, and
went to Egypt, and remained there until the death of Herod.
This was to fulfill what had been spoken by the Lord through
the prophet, "Out of Egypt I have called my son." When Herod
saw that he had been tricked by the wise men, he was infuri-
ated, and he sent and killed all the children in and around
Bethlehem who were two years old or under, according to
the time that he had learned from the wise men. Then was
fulfilled what had been spoken through the prophet Jeremiah:
"A voice was heard in Ramah,
wailing and loud lamentation,
Rachel weeping for her children;
she refused to be consoled,
because they are no more." Matthew 2:13–18

THE GOSPEL ACCORDING TO Matthew provides the only account of
the flight of Jesus with his parents to Egypt. At the time of Jesus'

birth, a large Jewish population lived in Egypt. Indeed, the Jewish philosopher Philo, a rough contemporary of Jesus, wrote that over a million Jews lived in Alexandria and elsewhere in Egypt around the time Jesus was born.

Matthew's narrative of the holy family fleeing to Egypt contrasts sharply with our last reading of response of joy at the birth of Jesus by the wise men from the East. Yet this darker side of the Christmas story resonates now, a time in history when the number of refugees is greater than ever.

Have you or your congregation helped sponsor refugees? What in their experience resembled that of Jesus and His family? How can we ensure the life, liberty and security of every person?

Prayer: Lord, we pray that we might love You and our neighbors as ourselves. May we remember those who may not be able to worship You, the lost and the lonely, the sick and those who sleep on streets, and refugees fleeing countries for reasons of fear, war or persecution. May we welcome them into our communities, as we welcome You into our hearts. Amen.

16

The Word Became Flesh

> In the beginning was the Word, and the Word was with God,
> and the Word was God. He was in the beginning with God. All
> things came into being through him, and without him not one
> thing came into being. What has come into being in him was
> life, and the life was the light of all people. The light shines in
> the darkness, and the darkness did not overcome it. John 1:1–5

LIKE MATTHEW, MARK AND Luke, John recounted scenes from Jesus' ministry. Many were miracles, such as turning water into wine at a wedding feast in Cana of Galilee (John 2:1–11), the healing of a man who had been ill for thirty-eight years (John 5:1–9) and feeding a hungry crowd of five thousand with only five barley loaves and two fish (John 6:1–15).

Also, John recorded teaching during which Jesus used familiar items of life According to John, Jesus said that He was the Bread of Life (John 6:35), the Light of the world (John 8:12), the Gate through which anyone who enters is saved (John 10:9) and the Good Shepard who lays down his life for his sheep (John 10:11).

As he began his account of the life and teachings of Jesus, John affirmed that Jesus was fully human, yet different from all other people. From the very beginning of creation, Jesus was with God. All things came into being through Him, and in Him was the light of all people. The light shone in the darkness and could not be overcome. In this way, John highlighted a mystery that is at the heart of the faith of Christians.

How might we respond to these miracles and words? Is the point of John to defend what scientists dispute? And atheists challenge? Or rather did John write his description of the life and teachings to strengthen our faith that through believing in Jesus, we have life in His name (John 20:11)?

Prayer: God, as I prepare to celebrate the birth of Jesus, may I give what I can, my heart and my praise all the day long. Amen.

17

Lamb of God

The next day he (John) saw Jesus coming toward him and declared, 'Here is the Lamb of God who takes away the sin of the world! This is he of whom I said, "After me comes a man who ranks ahead of me because he was before me." I myself did not know him; but I came baptizing with water for this reason, that he might be revealed to Israel.' And John testified . . . that "He on whom you see the Spirit descend and remain is the one who baptizes with the Holy Spirit." And I myself have seen and have testified that this is the Son of God.' John 1:29–34

SHEEP AND SHEPHERDS FIGURED prominently in the Psalms and in the ritual sacrifices of ancient Israel. In this text, John characterizes Jesus as "Lamb of God" and "Son of God." By these phrases, John sought to elicit faith. Following this passage, John affirms, "For God so loved the world that he gave his only Son, so that everyone who believes in him may not perish but may have eternal life." (John 3:16)

A crucial feature of this text is its reference to the Holy Spirit, who figures prominently throughout John's gospel. What do phrases like "Holy Spirit," "Lamb of God" or "Son of God" suggest to you? What qualities of a lamb come to your mind? Young? Innocent? Vulnerable? Food? Have you ever spoken of a small endearing child as lambkin? Do the description of Jesus as Lamb of God and Son of God contribute to your faith that, believing in Jesus, you may not perish but have eternal life? Have you ever struggled to believe that God can take care of you? As you reflect on today's text, I pray that you will be assured that God loves you and is with you on life's journey.

Prayer: God, awaken in me faith in You, love for You and certainty of Your presence today and always. Amen.

18

Blessed Are the Poor in Spirit

When Jesus saw the crowds, he went up the mountain; and
after he sat down, his disciples came to him. Then he began to
speak, and taught them, saying: Blessed are the poor in spirit,
for theirs is the kingdom of heaven. Matthew 5:1–3

ADVENT IS A SEASON of hope during the early days of winter when
the amount of daylight begins to lengthen. Today, we start a series
of reflection on the beatitudes as recorded in Matthew, with parallels in the other gospels. The beatitudes are part of Jesus' Sermon on
the Mount. Each begins with the word "blessed." Each consists of a
declaration of praise for an individual or group whose behavior is
regarded as exemplary and therefore receive God's favor.

Jesus proclaimed God's favor on those who are poor in spirt.
Who were these folk Jesus blessed? As suggested by prophet Micah
6:8, they were those who do justice, love mercy and walk humbly
before God. Jesus blessed them and assured them that they will inherit eternal life.

For me today, the poor in spirit are workers for peace, justice
and care of earth. Often persecuted by repressive regimes, they are
among those adopted by the human rights group Amnesty International. A simple phrase describes the impact of volunteers who
write letters and sign petitions on their behalf. "It is better to light a
candle than curse the darkness."

Who might you identify as poor in spirit? How might lighting a candle or writing a letter on his or her behalf be a benefit?

Prayer: Creator, Redeemer, Sustaining God, You have called us to be Your people in the world. We offer our lives to You in service of Your Realm of justice, peace and healing. Amen.

19

Blessed Are Those Who Mourn

> When Jesus saw the crowds, he went up the mountain; and
> after he sat down, his disciples came to him. Then he began
> to speak, and taught them, saying . . . blessed are those who
> mourn, for they will be comforted. Matthew 5: 1–2, 4

IN THE SECOND BEATITUDE, Jesus recognized that many present
might be mourning and need consolation or strengthening. In a
parallel text, Luke 6:21, Jesus said to his followers, "blessed are you
who weep now, for you will laugh."

Life is not always rosy. There are times when we feel at a
loss. This can especially be true in December, when daylight is at
a premium, holiday bills pile up and activity swirls into hectivity.
In addition to enjoying the glitter of Advent and Christmas, may
we also honor those who are feeling blue, especially those who
have recently lost a loved one. Many congregations organize a Blue
Holiday worship service in the hope of consoling those who have
recently experienced loss or displacement. By way of example,
MacNeill Baptist Church in Hamilton, Ontario, Canada used the
following litany and prayer on December 19, 2021.

> Gathering Litany: come to this place, you who are weary;
> it is waiting for you and all that you bring. We are here
> seeking respite from the expectations and demands of
> this season. Come to this place, you who long for a safe

haven; enter into the mystery of a holy presence. We are here with some hesitation, yet also with a longing to know peace and wholeness in the depth of our being. Come to this place, you who know the weight of loss; by grace the Creator is with you. We are here, waiting, and on the alert for God's voice to speak into our pain, into our hearts, into our lives. Wait for the Lord; be strong, and let your heart take courage. Our sadness and weeping is heard by others; our pain, loneliness, and loss are held close to the heart of God, who knows all that we feel.

Prayer: Creator God, lover of the universe, we come to you in this quiet place and time seeking your reassurance and your hope. We come in the midst of the noise, listening for your sustaining heartbeat. For those who are chilled by grief and pain, bring the warmth of your love. For those who are overwhelmed by feelings that exhaust and stifle, bring the cooling breeze of your love. We ask these things in the name of Jesus, born of a woman into a chaotic world of birth, death, and rebirth—just like today. Amen.

20

Blessed Are the Meek

> When Jesus saw the crowds, he went up the mountain; and
> after he sat down, his disciples came to him. Then he began to
> speak, and taught them, saying . . . blessed are the meek, for
> they will inherit the earth. Matthew 5: 1–2, 5

THIS BEATITUDE COMES FROM Psalm 37:11 and other passages that
express the virtue of meekness, or humility. In Biblical accounts, the
meek are those who rely on God. By contrast, the rich and powerful are often arrogant and proud. According to Jesus, God's realm
includes everyone, especially the meek.

Were Jesus alive today, who are the meek He might bless?
In a novel entitled *The Last Western,* Thomas A. Klise offers one
response. The novel's main character concerns Willie, an Irish-
Native American-Negro-Chinese boy who grows up in the slums
of Houston, Texas. Willie is entirely uneducable. However, he is
a magnificent baseball player. Consequently, it is not long before
scouts covet Willie who is soon pitching in the big leagues. Willie
quickly advances though the minor leagues. Astonishingly in his
first major league game, he strikes out twenty-seven consecutive
players, becoming an overnight sensation.

Sadly however, Willie soon realizes that the baseball execu-
tives are exploiting him. He becomes disillusioned with pro ball. At
this same time, urban America is convulsing in rioting and looting.

Willie returns home to find his family and friends have died in riots. His home has been razed. In horror, Willie flees and in despair runs and collapses outside the city. There, with his future seemingly helpless, he is found and nursed back to health by members of a group called the Silent Servants of the Used, Abused, and Utterly Screwed Up

Klise describes the Servants as followers of Jesus who always choose the way of serving the poor, the lonely, the despised, the outcast, the miserable and the misfit. The mission of the Servants is to prove to the unloved that they are not abandoned, nor ever left alone. The natural home of the Servants is strife, misfortune, crisis and the falling apart of things. They cherish failure for it is in failure, in trouble, in the general breaking up of classes, stations, usual conditions and natural routines that human hearts are open to the light of God's mercy.

Undoubtedly, Klise's Servants attend to the meek who in Jesus' beatitude inherit God's realm. Willie's story echoes Jesus' words in Matthew 25: 31–45 that when we feed the hungry, provide drink to those who thirst, welcome the stranger, clothe the naked or visit the imprisoned, we are caring for Jesus.

Prayer: God, in our world in which we encounter folk like Willie, help us remember that in responding to their needs, we are caring for You. Amen.

21

Hunger and Thirst after Righteousness

> He has told you, O mortal, what is good; and what does the
> Lord require of you but to do justice, and to love kindness, and
> to walk humbly with your God? Micah 6:8

> When Jesus saw the crowds, he went up the mountain; and
> after he sat down, his disciples came to him. Then he began
> to speak, and taught them, saying . . . Blessed are those who
> hunger and thirst for righteousness, for they will be filled.
> Matthew 5:1–2, 6

THE IDEA THAT A small number of persons who hunger and thirst after righteousness can save humankind is found in Genesis 6–8 where God chooses Noah, a "righteous man," to ensure that a remnant of humans as well as animals survive a great flood. In Genesis 19, the story of Sodom and Gomorrah, Abraham, patriarch of ancient Israel, negotiates with God not to destroy the wicked cities if ten righteous men lived there. Although ten were not found, the principle of the righteous few survives in the Jewish legend of the Thirty-Six Just. While the Thirty-Six do not realize their significance, their prayers and actions become the pillars that support the earth and prevent its destruction.

The prophet Micah writes that God wants us to do justice, to be compassionate and to walk humbly with God. As well, Jesus blesses those who seek righteousness. And according to James 3:18, the harvest of righteousness is sown in peace for those who make peace.

These texts highlight that God calls us to act justly, love kindly and walk humbly. Jesus blesses those who hunger and thirst after righteousness. Can you identify someone whose actions and prayers really matter? In what way has his or her search for righteousness been satisfied?

Prayer: God, may I be mindful of Your presence in those around me. Enable me so to hunger and thirst after righteousness that You satisfy my deepest yearning. Amen.

22

Blessed Are the Merciful

> When Jesus saw the crowds, he went up the mountain; and
> after he sat down, his disciples came to him. Then he began
> to speak, and taught them, saying . . . Blessed are the merciful,
> for they will receive mercy. Matthew 5:1–2

> When the Pharisees heard that he had silenced the Sadducees,
> they gathered together, and one of them, a lawyer, asked him
> a question to test him. "Teacher, which commandment in
> the law is the greatest?" He said to him, "'You shall love the
> Lord your God with all your heart, and with all your soul, and
> with all your mind.' This is the greatest and first command-
> ment. And a second is like it: 'You shall love your neighbor as
> yourself.' On these two commandments hang all the law and
> the prophets." Matthew 22:34–40

TODAY'S READING FROM THE Sermon on the Mount reveals God as forgiving and merciful. Thus when Jesus passed along the shore of the Sea of Galilee, He then ascended a mountain where huge crowds had gathered. There, many disabled individuals, including the lame, maimed, blind and mute approached Jesus begging to be healed. Jesus cured them and explained, "I have compassion for the crowd, because they have been with me now for three days and have nothing to eat, and I do not want to send them away hungry. . ." (Matthew 15:32 and parallels).

Throughout the four gospels, Jesus made God's mercy tangible. His mercy was not abstract, but concrete. Jesus' Great Commandment to love God and our neighbor as ourselves summarized His basic teaching.

We who follow Jesus are similarly to be merciful. We are blessed and receive mercy. An example of such a ministry is that of John Perkins, emeritus pastor of Voice of Calvary Ministries in Jackson, Mississippi. Once in Memphis, Tennessee, he explained, "The church should be a port, not a fort."

By this I understood that a congregation does not exist to bring together folk for an hour on Sunday morning, but rather to enable Christians to live the Great Commandment, daily sharing God's love and mercy with all. Who come to mind when you think of such merciful persons? Are they forgiving? Do they listen? Do they empower others to follow Jesus' teachings? How can you help people hear Jesus' words teaching and respond to His life-changing message?

Let us close with a prayer originally by Richard, Bishop of Chichester in 1253, and adapted from the musical *Godspell*, Dear Lord, I pray three things, that daily I may see You more clearly, love You more dearly and follow You more nearly. I pray in Jesus's name. Amen.

23

Blessed Are the Pure in Heart

> When Jesus saw the crowds, he went up the mountain; and
> after he sat down, his disciples came to him. Then he began
> to speak, and taught them, saying . . . Blessed are the pure in
> heart, for they will see God. Matthew 5:1–2, 8

IN THIS BEATITUDE AND the verses that follow. Jesus was concerned
that, when you give an offering, pray, or fast, you do so sincerely,
free from expecting to be praised by others. When you participate
in such devotional practices, Jesus counseled that you do so with
purity of heart for only then will you see God.

Purity of Heart Is To Will One Thing is the title of a devotional
classic by Søren Kierkegaard, a nineteenth-century Danish thinker
who urged Christians to worship God without pretense or false
piety. Kierkegaard called upon readers to abandon old securities
and to build new foundations for faith by confessing one's sins and
willing the good.

Are there times when you have experienced someone who
makes a pretense of sincerity yet whose deeds are not obviously
congruent with his or her words? How do you feel when you greet
someone who says, "Hello. How are you?" yet openly signals disin-
terest in your welfare? Under such circumstance, can you respond
in a truthful manner?

Let us pray with words adapted from Kierkegaard's book: Father in Heaven, You alone are holy. You alone are with me as the day waxes and wanes. I repent my sins and thank You for Your forgiveness. Give me the courage to will one thing, to follow You in my daily tasks. When I lay down to rest, grant me a good night's rest that I may awaken to another day in Your care. Amen.

24

Blessed Are the Peacemakers

> When Jesus saw the crowds, he went up the mountain; and after he sat down, his disciples came to him. Then he began to speak, and taught them, saying . . . Blessed are the peacemakers, for they will be called children of God. Matthew 5:1–2, 9

PEACE IS A COMPLEX word. In the *Bible*, peace signifies absence of conflict, conditions for a just world and a process by which one endeavors to achieve it. The phrase "seek peace and pursue it" (Psalm 34:14), suggests two dimensions of peacemaking. The first is visionary: seeking a better world in which injustice, violence and war no longer exist. The second is practical: finding common ground for resolving conflict through peaceful means like conciliation and arbitration.

I have long opposed a false historical perception that Christians generally are not peacemakers. In Hamilton, Ontario, Canada where I currently reside, I have identified with a group dedicated to peacebuilding who have called on people everywhere to reduce violence and cultivate peace in their own neighborhoods. Understanding that everyone can contribute to peacemaking, we have worked diligently to apply these principles locally and also to spread them beyond our community. As a framework for social justice, we have identified six pathways for peacemakers: respect all life;

reject violence; share with others; listen to understand: preserve the planet and rediscover solidarity.

Over time, the group has had a number of successes, such as creating a peace garden at Hamilton city hall and supporting peace studies at McMaster University. Similarly, like throwing a stone into still water, members of the local chapter of Amnesty International join hundreds of volunteers worldwide on behalf of a prisoner of conscience in a global movement to respect human rights. Thus, the message is clear from these actions: each of us is a peacemaker, contributing in our own context to promoting the greater common good.

Prayer: Almighty and Merciful God, Creator and Redeemer, we seek your peace in our lives, and in the lives of others. As peacemakers, may we be angels bearing good news of Your mercy and Your peace for all. Amen.

25

Blessed Are Those Who are Persecuted

When Jesus saw the crowds, he went up the mountain; and after he sat down, his disciples came to him. Then he began to speak, and taught them, saying . . . Blessed are those who are persecuted for righteousness' sake, for theirs is the kingdom of heaven. Blessed are you when people revile you and persecute you and utter all kinds of evil against you falsely on my account. Rejoice and be glad, for your reward is great in heaven, for in the same way they persecuted the prophets who were before you. Matthew 5:1–2, 10–12

IN THE LAST OF the beatitudes, Jesus spoke about those in authority punishing those who outwardly oppressed them, or were suspected of opposing them. Mighty kings persecuted prophets who lamented the fate of the common people. Jews suffered at the hands of Egyptian and, later, Roman rulers. The persecution of Jews often took the form of hostility by an angry crowd, loss of civil and religious rights, imprisonment, torture or death.

Jesus blessed those who were persecuted for righteousness' sake. Indeed, this was to be Jesus' fate and likewise that of many of His followers who spread His teachings long after His death.

Numerous books and hymns have kept alive the memories of righteous individuals who have suffered from such persecution.

Readers who tour the Holy Land visit Calvary, a hill in biblical Jerusalem where Jesus was crucified and Masada high atop cliffs overlooking the Dead Sea that was the site of the last stand of Jewish patriots in the face of the Roman army in 73 A.D. Similarly, to cite an example from near my home, many pilgrims visit Martyrs' Shrine near Midland, Ontario. This was where Jean de Brébeuf, composer of *'Twas in the Moon of Wintertime*, and his Christian companions were brutally tortured and killed in the mid-seventeenth century.

Can you name someone who has been persecuted for his or her faithful witness? Perhaps you can think of a time when you felt persecuted or falsely accused on account of your faith. If so, surely you are blessed by the Almighty and will enter the kingdom of heaven.

Prayer: God, we give thanks for Jesus, and for faithful witnesses to His life and teachings. We remember what upholding righteousness cost Him and His early followers. Amen.

26

The Lord's Prayer

Pray then in this way: Our Father in heaven, hallowed be your
name. Your kingdom come. Your will be done, on earth as it
is in heaven. Give us this day our daily bread. And forgive us
our debts, as we also have forgiven our debtors. And do not
bring us to the time of trial, but rescue us from the evil one.

Matthew 6:9–13

IN THE MIDDLE AGES, a book entitled *The Cloud of Unknowing*
taught a form of prayer in three movements. First, settle into a place
conducive for silence, solitude and stillness. It can be anywhere.
Virtually every home has a place where no one will disturb you. In
my case, my partner Nancy and I set aside a few minutes most days
in a room from which we look out upon a valley below our home.
We light a candle, identify prayer concerns then sit quietly for a few
minutes.

The medieval writer then suggests concentrating on a single-
syllable word such as God, joy, love or peace. The word should reflect God in all the divine fullness to you. Simply let this word and
nothing else hold sway in your mind or heart during this time of
meditation.

Finally, one may read from a book of prayers, or one of the
Psalms, perhaps in contemporary editions such as Leslie F. Brant's

Psalms Now or Jim Cotter's *Out of the Silence . . . Into the Silence. Prayer's Daily Round.* The Psalms continue to have amazing authenticity. By their expression of a full range of human emotions, including anguish, elation, rage and praise, the Psalms are a vital companion on our faith journey.

Christians likely know no scripture better than The Lord's Prayer. Long before we voice this prayer, God knows our need for daily bread, forgiveness and strength to endure the trials of life. By choosing to articulate these essential areas of living, we express our desire to walk a path of humility, holiness and boldness with our God. If comfortable, I invite readers of this collection to spend their devotional time today in one of several ways. One suggestion is to pray the Lord's Prayer sentence by sentence. Leave a few moments or minutes after each phrase to express the thoughts the words elicit. Another possibility is to consider singing or listening to a musical setting of the prayer. A third alternative is praying a modern version. One example is from *A New Zealand Prayer Book*, as follows:

> Eternal Spirit, Earth-maker, Pain-bearer, Life-giver, Source of all that is and that shall be, Father and Mother of us all, Loving God, in whom is heaven: The hallowing of your name echo through the universe! The way of your justice be followed by the peoples of the world! Your heavenly will be done by all created beings! Your commonwealth of peace and freedom sustain our hope and come on earth. With the bread we need for today, feed us. In the hurts we absorb from one another, forgive us. In times of temptation and testing, strengthen us. From trials too great to endure, spare us. From the grip of all that is evil, free us. For you reign in the glory of the power that is love, now and forever. Amen.

In *The Message*, Biblical scholar Eugene H. Peterson offered the following paraphrase:

> With a God like this loving you, you can pray very simply. Our Father in heaven, Reveal who you are. Set the world right; Do what's best—as above, so below. Keep us alive with three square meals. Keep us forgiven with you and forgiving others. Keep us safe from ourselves and the

Devil. You're in charge! You can do anything you want!
You're ablaze in beauty! Yes. Yes. Yes.

In 1942, Biblical scholar Clarence Jordan co-founded an inter-
racial Christian community in Americus, Georgia, where a group
of extraordinary disciples lived their faith without fear of the con-
sequences. Jordan translated The Lord's Prayer in southern idiom.
Here is his rendering:

> Father of us, O Spiritual One, Your Name be truly hon-
> ored. Your Movement spread, your will prevail through
> earth, as through the heavens. Grant us sustaining bread
> each day. Forgive our debts, as we forgive the debts of
> all who cannot pay. And from confusion keep us clear;
> deliver us from evil's sway. Amen

27

Love One Another

When the Pharisees heard that Jesus had silenced the
Sadducees, they gathered together, and one of them, a lawyer,
asked him a question to test him. "Teacher, which commandment in the law is the greatest?" He said to him, "You shall love
the Lord your God with all your heart, with all your soul, and
with all your mind. This is the greatest and first commandment. And a second is like it: You shall love your neighbor as
yourself. On these two commandments hang all the law and
the prophets." Matthew 22:34–40

LOVE GOD. LOVE YOUR neighbor. Love yourself. Jesus thus summarizes the law of love, which He illustrated by example throughout
His ministry, even unto His death. Loving God, oneself and one
another not only sums up Jesus' teaching, but also that of the apostle
Paul. Highlighting the commandment to love one another in his letter to the Romans, chapter 13:8–12, Paul affirms that we owe no one
anything except our love. The reader of this booklet who so loves
God, others and him- or herself has thus fulfilled the law of love.

Christians have given witness to this divine love through the
ages. Let me cite several examples. First, the eighteenth-century
British poet and artist William Blake summarizes the law of love as
follows: "I sought my God and my God I could not find. I sought

my soul and my soul eluded me. I sought my brother to serve him in his need, and I found all three—my God, my soul, and thee."

Second, in June 1964, Trappist monk Thomas Merton traveled to New York City to meet Zen master Daisetz. T. Suzuki. After the two men had meditated and drank tea together, Suzuki's last words to Merton were, "The most important thing is Love."

Third, in a Christmas hymn, the English-born poet of Italian parentage Christina G. Rossetti wrote that love came down at Christmas, all lovely and divine. How did she know this? Rosetti confidently answered that the stars and angels had given her the sign.

Finally, a popular hymn celebrates that Jesus loves us. How do we know? Because, as the words of the hymn continue, the *Bible* tells us so.

Prayer: God, empowered by Your Spirit, may we love You and our neighbors as ourselves. Amen.

28

Friends of Jesus

This is my commandment, that you love one another as I have
loved you. No one has greater love than this, to lay down one's
life for one's friends. You are my friends if you do what I com-
mand you. I do not call you servants any longer, because the
servant does not know what the master is doing; but I have
called you friends, because I have made known to you everything that I have heard from my Father. You did not choose
me but I chose you. And I appointed you to go and bear fruit,
fruit that will last, so that the Father will give you whatever
you ask him in my name. I am giving you these commands so
that you may love one another. John 15:12–17

JESUS CALLED HIS IMMEDIATE followers friends. These friends
formed a redeemed community tasked with spreading the teaching
of Jesus to all humanity. In a book entitled *For the Inward Journey*,
Baptist pastor and university chaplain Howard Thurman empha-
sized the "brooding Presence of the Eternal Spirit" in a Christmas
reflection, as follows:

> The symbol of Christmas . . . is the rainbow arched over
> the world of the sky when the clouds are heavy with fore-
> boding. It is the cry of life in the newborn babe when,
> forced from its mother's nest, it claims its right to live.

It is the brooding Presence of the Eternal Spirit making crooked paths straight, rough places smooth, tired hearts refreshed, dead hopes stirred with the newness of life. It is the promise of tomorrow at the close of every day, the movement of life in defiance of death, and the assurance that love is sturdier than hate, that right is more confident than wrong, that good is more permanent than evil.

Thurman also wrote of lighting candles of friendship at Christmas. He expressed the hope that these candles might burn all year long.

In a world dominated by science, technology, the drive to acquire power for its own sake, materialism and consumerism, we need to remember friends of Jesus who demonstrate the love of God in their daily lives, without fanfare or neon lights. Can you name a friend of Jesus who has helped the movement of life in defiance of death? In what way is he or she a friend with Jesus?

Prayer: Loving God, this Christmas we thank You for the gift of friends. Symbolically, we light a candle of friendship with You. This is a candle of hope that will burn this coming year. Amen.

29

Bearers of the Divine Image

His divine power has given us everything needed for life and godliness, through the knowledge of him who called us by his own glory and goodness. Thus he has given us, through these things, his precious and very great promises, so that through them you may escape from the corruption that is in the world because of lust, and may become participants of the divine nature. For this very reason, you must make every effort to support your faith with goodness, and goodness with knowledge, and knowledge with self-control, and self-control with endurance, and endurance with godliness, and godliness with mutual affection, and mutual affection with love. For if these things are yours and are increasing among you, they keep you from being ineffective and unfruitful in the knowledge of our Lord Jesus Christ. For anyone who lacks these things is near-sighted and blind, and is forgetful of the cleansing of past sins. Therefore, brothers and sisters, be all the more eager to confirm your call and election, for if you do this, you will never stumble. For in this way, entry into the eternal kingdom of our Lord and Savior Jesus Christ will be richly provided for you. 2 Peter 1:3–11

I WAS BAPTIZED AND initially raised in the Russian Orthodox Church, the religious tradition of my biological father and grandparents. From an early age, I knew Christian practices differed such as the date on which Christmas is celebrated. For example, though no one really knows the date of Jesus's birth, some Christians celebrate on December 25th and others on January 7th.

Since we followed the Julian calendar, which is older than the one used in the west today, we attended a service the morning of January 7. After the worship, a priest sometimes came to our home to offer a blessing. Since many relatives had fasted for a few days, the Christmas meal was a grand feast, with such traditional Russian dishes as beet salad, borscht, boiled potatoes with onions, piroshky and pelimeni, a dumpling filled with meat or fish. A white tablecloth symbolized purity and the fabric in which Mary wrapped Jesus.

While specific practices vary by culture and religious tradition, what really matters, according to today's reading, is that, as sons and daughters of the living God, we reflect this inner reality that, created in the image and likeness of God, we are bearers of the Holy One. We practice our faith with goodness, knowledge, self-control, endurance, godliness, mutual affection and love.

Let us close with a prayer from the Orthodox Christian tradition: Heavenly King, the Comforter, the Spirit of truth, present everywhere and filling all things, treasury of blessings and giver of life, come and abide in us. Cleanse us from every stain and save our souls, gracious Lord. Amen.

30

The Little Mandate

Now when Jesus came into the district of Caesarea Philippi,
he asked his disciples, "Who do people say that the Son of
Man is?" And they said, "Some say John the Baptist, but others
Elijah, and still others Jeremiah or one of the prophets." He
said to them, "But who do you say that I am?" Simon Peter
answered, "You are the Messiah, the Son of the living God."
. . .Then Jesus told his disciples, "If any want to become my
followers, let them deny themselves and take up their cross
and follow me. For those who want to save their life will
lose it, and those who lose their life for my sake will find it.
For what will it profit them if they gain the whole world but
forfeit their life? Or what will they give in return for their
life?" Matthew 16:13–16, 24–26

AT THE END OF His life, Jesus asked His disciples who they thought
He was. Peter replied, "You are the Messiah, the Son of the living
God." Jesus responded by blessing Peter and charging His disciples
to deny themselves and to follow Him. Read with other texts, Jesus'
call to follow Him has profound implications for us living in the
early twenty-first century.

Among Christians who have mirrored for me what following Jesus entails, Catherine de Hueck Doherty was a Russian

immigrant first to New York City. Early in the twentieth century, she then settled at Combermere, near Ottawa, Ontario, Canada where she helped establish Madonna House, a Christian community that serves the rural poor along with sister groups and inspires many Christians to follow in the path of discipleship taught by Jesus. Doherty summarizes key principles of Madonna House in "The Little Mandate" as follows:

> Arise—go! Sell all you possess. Give it directly, personally to the poor. Take up my cross (their cross) and follow Me, going to the poor, being poor, being one with them, one with Me. Little—be always little! Be simple, poor, and childlike. Preach the Gospel with your life—*without compromise*! Listen to the Spirit. He will lead you. Do little things exceedingly well for love of Me. Love. . .love. . .love, never counting the cost. Go into the marketplace and stay with Me. Pray, fast. Pray always, fast. Be hidden. Be a light to your neighbor's feet. Go without fears into the depth of men's hearts. I shall be with you. Pray always. I will be your rest.

What do experience as you read these words? What prayer can you offer in response?

31

Wishes and Intentions

AFTER JOURNEYING THROUGH ADVENT and Christmas, many Christians then make New Year Resolutions that highlight intentions for the coming year. Our wishes and intentions are personal and often involve praying for the greater common good. Some organizations, such as the Make-A-Wish Foundation, highlight life-affecting wishes for children battling critical illnesses which can give families hope through dark times, strength to persevere and joy that forever changes their lives.

In her collection of twelve Christmas miracles, Joan Rattner Heilman writes about twelve Christmas miracles that really happened. One of particular interest to me concerns six-year old Michael Klein while he was sitting on Santa Claus's lap. When asked by jolly old St. Nick, "How are you son?" Michael answered. "Fine." "And what would you like for Christmas?" Santa continued. "Well, I'd like a dog and a fire engine and. . ." His list was long. What was most unusual about their conversation was that Michael talked.

Now why was that a miracle you might ask? Well, although Michael had begun to speak at a normal age, a few years later. Suddenly and seemingly without explanation, he stopped talking for many years. Somehow, while offering wishes at Christmas, Michael regained his ability to speak.

What wishes and intentions do you have this New Year's Eve. Years ago, on the eve of a New Millennium, December 31, 1999,

His Holiness Tenzin Gyatso, the fourteenth Dalai Lama and exiled leader of Tibetan Buddhism invited reflection as follows:

1. How do we address the widening gap between rich and poor?
2. How do we protect the earth?
3. How do we educate our children?
4. How do we help oppressed countries and peoples of the world?
5. How do we bring spirituality (deep caring for one another) through all of life.

He then said that the answers to all five questions could be found in the last one. If we have compassion in our hearts, we will be led to look after others, ensure children are educated wisely, care for earth and address the needs of those who "have not." Someone then asked, "Do you think loving on the planet is increasing or staying the same?" The Dalai Lama replied that his experience led him to believe that love and compassion were increasing throughout the world, and that this could herald a greater understanding among all people and more respect for the earth, our home.

Today on the eve of a new year, do you find that these questions challenging? Have these meditations helped you focus on the true meaning of Christmas? What are your intentions for next year? As we conclude today's meditation, a carol "Christmas Wishes" highlights my three wishes. If these are granted, in a world no less troubled than that into which Jesus was born, there will truly be peace on earth, good will among all people and love in all that we do.

Prayer: O God, You have called me to journey with You in humble ways, helping to share Good News with others. Open my eyes to Your care for me, and grant me the grace of Your power to trust in Your love, guidance and protection. I pray in Jesus' name. Amen.

Further Reading

A Manual of Eastern Orthodox Prayers. London: SPCK, 1945

A New Zealand Prayer Book. San Francisco: HarperCollins, 1989

Appleton, George, ed. *The Oxford Book of Prayer.* Oxford: Oxford University Press, 1988

———. *Jerusalem Prayers for the World Today.* London: SPCK, 1974

Ashmankas, Brian and Vicki Lott. *The Time to Be Awake. Reflections for Advent & Christmas.* Washington, D. C.: Pax Christi USA, 2019

Auden, W. H. "Christmas Oratio." https://southerncrossreview.org/44/auden-oratio.htm

Bainton, Roland H., ed. *The Martin Luther Christmas Book with Celebrated Woodcuts by His Contemporaries.* Philadelphia: Fortress, 1948

Brant, Leslie F. *Psalms Now.* St. Louis: Concordia, 1973

Buber, Martin. *I and Thou,* translated by Walter Kaufmann. New York: Charles Scribner's Sons, 1970

Buttrick, George Arthur, ed. *The Interpreter's Dictionary of the Bible,* 4 vols. Nashville: Abingdon, 1962

Coren, Michael, *The Rebel Christ.* Toronto: Dundurn, 2021

Cotter, Jim. *Psalms for a Pilgrim People.* Harrisburg: Morehouse, 1998

Davey, Ray. *A Chanel of Peace.* Toronto: HarperCollins Canada, 1993

Dekar, Paul R. *Baptists Are Not Peacemakers,* "Baptist Myths." Brentwood: Baptist History and Heritage Society, 2003

———. *Community of the Transfiguration. Journey of a New Monastic Community.* Eugene: Cascade, 2008

———. *For the Healing of the Nations. Baptist Peacemakers.* Macon: Smyth and Helwys, 1993

———. *Holy Boldness. Practices of an Evangelistic Lifestyle.* Macon: Smyth and Helwys, 2004

———. *Thomas Merton: God's Messenger on the Road towards a New World.* Eugene: Cascade, 2021

———. *Thomas Merton. Twentieth Century Wisdom for Twenty-First Century Living.* Eugene: Cascade, 2011

Doherty, Catherine de Hueck, *Essential Writings*, edited by David Meconi. Maryknoll: Orbis, 2009

Douglas, Mary. *Purity and Danger: An Analysis of Concepts of Pollution and Taboo*. Harmondsworth: Penguin, 1966

Dozier, Verna J. *The Dream of God. A Call to Return*. Cambridge: Cawley, 1991

Elliot, T. S. *The Complete Poems and Plays* 1909–1950. New York: Harcourt, Brace and World, 1962

Ellsberg, Robert. *All Saints. Daily Reflections on Saints, Prophets, and Witnesses for Our Time*. New York: Crossroad, 1997

Esdale, Jane, introduction. *Think on These Things. Meditations for December*. Charlotte: Baptist Peace Fellowship of North America, 2002

Falla, Terry C. *Be Our Freedom Lord*. Adelaide: Open Book, 1994

Ferguson, Ron, ed. *Daily Readings with George Macleod*. London: Fount, 1991

Ghosh, Amitav. *The Nutmeg's Curse. Parables for a Planet in Crisis*. Chicago: University of Chicago Press, 2021

Glen, Genevieve. *Daily Reflections for Advent and Christmas. Waiting in Joyful Hope* 2018–19. Collegeville: Liturgical, 2018

Heilman, Joan Rattner, "Twelve Christmas Miracles that Really Happened," *Family Life*, December 11, 1979, pp. 126–137

Jenner, Brian, et al. *Gentle Angry People. Songs of Protest and Praise*. Stafford: Alliance of Radical Methodists, 1987

Jordan, Clarence. *The Cotton Patch Version of Matthew and John*. New York: Association, 1970

Julian of Norwich. *Showings*, translated by Edmund College and James Walsh. New York: Paulist, 1978

Kadas, Sotiris. *Mount Athos. An Illustrated Guide to the Monasteries and Their History*. Athens: Ekdotike Ahtenon, 1979

Kierkegaard, Søren. *Purity of Heart Is To Will One Thing*, translated by Douglas V. Steere. New York: Harper & Row, 1948.

Klise, Thomas A. *The Last Western*. Niles: Argus Communications, 1974

Kurelek, William. *A Northern Nativity. Christmas Dreams of a Prairie Boy*. Montreal: Tundra, 1976

Lee, Dallas, *The Cotton Patch Evidence. The Story of Clarence Jordan and the Koinonia Farm Experiment*. New York: Harper & Row, 1971

Machado, Antonio. "XXIX," *Border of a Dream: Selected Poems* https://www.goodreads.com/author/quotes/34610.Antonio_Machado

Merton, Thomas. *Essential Writings*, edited by Christine M. Bochen. Maryknoll: Orbis, 2001

———. *Thoughts in Solitude*. New York: Farrar, Straus, Giroux, 1956; for a prayer by Merton read by the late Matthew Kelty, https://www.youtube.com/watch?v=BFTniXnoZCM

Momaday, N. Scott. *Circle of Wonder. A Native American Christmas Story*. Albuquerque: University of New Mexico, 1994

The New Oxford Annotated Bible, New Revised Standard Version. New York: Oxford University Press, 1991

Nouwen, Henri J. M. *The Genesee Diary: Report from a Trappist Monastery.* Garden City: Doubleday, 1976

O'Connor, Elizabeth. *Call to Commitment. The Story of the Church of the Saviour. Washington, D. C.* New York: Harper & Row, 1963

———. *Journey Inward, Journey Outward.* New York: HarperCollins, 1975

O'Connor, Jerome Murphy. *The Holy Land. An Archaeological Guide from the Earliest Times to 1700.* Oxford: Oxford University Press, 1980

O'Neil. Dan. *Signatures. The Story of John Michael Talbot.* Barryville: Troubladour for the Lord, 2003

Perkins, John, M. *Resurrecting Hope.* Ventura: Regal, 1995

Peterson, Eugene H. *The Message. The Bible in Contemporary Language.* Colorado Springs: NavPress, 2002

Robinson, Barbara. *The Best Christmas Pageant Ever.* New York: Harper/ Collins, 2011

The Rule of St. Benedict in English, ed. Timothy Fry. Collegeville: Liturgical, 1982

Rutba House. *School(s) for Conversion: 12 Marks of a New Monasticism.* Eugene: Cascade, 2005

Saint-Exupéry, *The Little Prince*, translated by Katherine Woods. New York: Harcourt, Brace & World, 1943

Schwarz-Barr, André. *The Last of the Just*, translated by Stephen Becker. New York: Bantam, 1960

Steere, Douglas V. *Bethlehem Revisited.* Pamphlet 144. Wallingford: Pendle Hill, 1965

Talmud, 10 Shevat 5735, https://www.chabad.org/therebbe/livingtorah/player_cdo/aid/618981/jewish/A-Candle-for-One-A-Light-for-All.htm

Tantur Papers on Christianity in the Holy Land. Jerusalem: Ecumenical Institute for Theological Research, 1981

Thurman, Howard. *For the Inward Journey. The Writings of Howard Thurman* selected by Anne Spencer Thurman. Richmond: Friends United Meeting, 1984

MUSIC

de Brébeuf, Jean, "'Twas in the Moon of Wintertime"

Carpenter, Mary Chapin, "Jubilee," *Stones on the Rock*

Campbell, Kate, "Thomas Merton's Prayer," *For the Living of These Days*, https://www.youtube.com/watch?v=8QO2hCpb3Uk

Cotter, Jim, *Out of the Silence . . . Into the Silence. Prayer's Daily Round* with music composed by Paul Payton. Harlech: Cairns, 2006

Handel, George Frederic, *Messiah*

New Christie Minstrels. "Christmas Wishes" *https://www.youtube.com/watch?v=qseAL_1wf_I&list=RDqseAL_1wf_I&index=2*

Praying Together in Word and Song, Taizé Community. London and Oxford: Mowbray, 1988.

Taizé Cantante!

Talbot, John Michael, *Signatures*, 2003

The Presbyterian Hymnal: Hymns, Psalms, and Spiritual Songs. Louisville: Westminster/John Knox Press, 1990

Voices United. The Hymn and Worship Book of the United Church of Canada. Etobicoke: United Church of Canada, 1996

USA Africa, *We Are the World*, 1985

Winter, Miriam Therese, *An Anthology of Scripture Songs*. Philadelphia: Medical Missionary Sisters, 1982

MONASTERIES AND RETREAT CENTERS

Abbey of Gethsemani, Trappist, Kentucky. https://www.trappists.org/gethsemani -abbey/.

Other Trappist monasteries of the Order of Cistercians of the Strict Observance include Genesee Abbey in Pifford, New York; Guadalupe Abbey in Lafayette, Oregon; and Tarrawarra Abbey near Melbourne in Victoria, Australia.

Church of the Saviour, Washington, D. C. https://en.wikipedia.org/wiki/ Church_of_the_Saviour_%28Washington,_D.C.%29

Corrymeela Community, Northern Ireland. https://www.corrymeela.org/ about/our-history

Holy Transfiguration Monastery near Melbourne, with associates in Canada, England and United States, is a ministry of Australian Baptist Ministries. https://www.baptist.org.au/

Iona Community, Island of Iona, Scotland, is ecumenical with associates around the world. https://www.ionacommunity.com/

Ignatius House near Guelph, Ontario, takes the order's name, Ignatius of Loyola. https://ignatiusguelph.ca/loyola-house/

Little Portion Hermitage and Monastery, Berryville, Arkansas is Franciscan with associates around the world. https://bscdomestic.org/little-portion- hermitage

Madonna House, Combermere, Ontario, is Catholic and incorporates Russian Orthodox spirituality of co-founder Catharine de Hueck Doherty. https:// www.madonnahouse.org/

Rutba House, Walltown, Durham, North Carolina, is part of a network of New Monastic Communities. https://www.schoolforconversion.org/about-us

Sisters of Loretto, Nerinx, Kentucky; https://www.youtube.com/watch?v=fo AhD4Jo8CU

St. John's Abbey, Collegeville, Minnesota and Saint Benedict's Monastery, St. Joseph, Minnesota are Benedictine. https://saintjohnsabbey.org/ and https://sbm.osb.org/

In Greece, Mount Athos admits men only. https://www.monastiriaka.gr/en/ visit-mount-athos—-pilgrims-office—-diamonitirio-n-23524.html.

As elsewere, in southern Ontario, where I live, numerous communities offer worship or retreats. https://hamiltondiocese.com/vocations/religious-conse crated-life.php or
https://www.archtoronto.org/siteassets/media/offices—ministries/administrative -offices/spiritual-affairs/files/orderhierarchywomen2021.pdf

www.ingramcontent.com/pod-product-compliance
Lightning Source LLC
LaVergne TN
LVHW050047090426
835511LV00033B/2775